JAMESTOWN  EDUCATION

# In the Spotlight
## Volume 2

**Levels D–F**

**Henry Billings**

**Melissa Billings**

 Glencoe

New York, New York    Columbus, Ohio    Chicago, Illinois    Peoria, Illinois    Woodland Hills, California

JAMESTOWN EDUCATION

Glencoe

The *McGraw·Hill* Companies

ISBN-13: 978-0-07-874323-8
ISBN-10: 0-07-874323-0

Send all queries to:
Glencoe/McGraw-Hill
8787 Orion Place
Columbus, OH 43240-4027

3 4 5 6 7 8 9 10  021  10 09 08

# Contents

# Unit Three

# To the Student

This book has nine articles about celebrities, or famous people, in the world today. Some of the celebrities are movie or television stars. Some are sports players. Others are authors or musicians.

The lives of these stars can inspire us. Some of the stars had tough times while growing up. They worked very hard to find success. Others had to stay focused on their dreams even when other people thought they would fail. And some had to get through challenges even after they became well-known.

In this book you will work on these three specific reading skills:

**Using Context**
**Cause and Effect**
**Making Predictions**

You will also work on other reading and vocabulary skills. This will help you understand and think about what you read. The lessons include types of questions often found on state and national tests. Completing the questions can help you get ready for tests you may have to take later.

# How to Use This Book

## About the Book

This book has three units. Each unit has three lessons. Each lesson has an article about a celebrity followed by practice exercises.

## Working Through Each Lesson

**Photo** Start each lesson by looking at the photo. Read the title and subtitle to get an idea of what the article will focus on.

**Think About What You Know, Word Power, Reading Skill** This page will help you prepare to read.

**Article** Now read about the celebrity. Enjoy!

**Activities** Complete all the activities. Then check your work. Your teacher will give you an answer key to do this. Record the number of your correct answers for each activity. At the end of the lesson, add up your total score for parts A, B, and C. Then find your percentage score in the table. Record your percentage score on the Comprehension and Critical Thinking Progress Graph on page 105.

**Compare and Contrast Chart** At the end of each unit, you will complete a Compare and Contrast Chart. The chart will help you see what some of the celebrities in the unit have in common.

**My Personal Dictionary** In the back of this book, you can jot down words you would like to know more about. Later you can ask your teacher or a classmate what the words mean. Then you can add the definitions in your own words.

Ricky Martin

Ellen MacArthur

Bethany Hamilton

# Ricky Martin
## Performing Since Childhood

**Birth Name** Enrique José Martin Morales IV
**Birth Date and Place** December 24, 1971; San Juan, Puerto Rico
**Home** Miami Beach, Florida

# Think About What You Know

Is there a famous person who inspires you? What is inspiring about this person? Read the article to find out how Ricky Martin inspires fans with his music and his giving.

# Word Power

What do the words below tell you about the article?

**electrified** surprised and thrilled

**rehearsing** practicing for a performance, such as a concert

**anthem** a song that praises something, such as a team or a country

**surge** a sudden rise

**meditate** to relax and become more aware of yourself, often done while sitting with eyes closed

# Reading Skill

**Using Context** **Context clues** can help you find the meaning of a word that you don't understand. Context clues are other words in the same sentence or in nearby sentences. If you don't understand a word, look for clues around it that might help you. Then try to find the meaning.

**Example**

My brother and his friends started their own band. They are going to give a concert for the whole neighborhood. I

**New Word**

am in charge of publicity for the concert. I made posters

**Context Clues**

and put them up all around the neighborhood. I want to make sure everyone knows about the concert.

If you don't know the meaning of the word *publicity,* you can use the context clues "I made posters and put them up" and "make sure everyone knows" to help you find the meaning. From these clues, what do you think *publicity* means?

3

# Ricky Martin
## Performing Since Childhood

February 24, 1999, was a night Ricky Martin would never forget. The biggest stars in music had gathered in Los Angeles for the 41st annual Grammy Awards. Millions of TV viewers had tuned in to watch. While some of them had heard of Ricky Martin, he wasn't really considered a big star. People began to think of him differently, however, when Martin walked out on stage and gave a live performance of his song "La Copa de la Vida" ("The Cup of Life").

2   The song lasted only 210 seconds, but in that short time Martin **electrified** the audience. Until then the awards show had been pretty dull. Martin's performance made people stand up and cheer. Suddenly Ricky Martin was one of the hottest performers in the United States.

3   By summer Martin had another song at the top of the charts. It was called "Livin' la Vida Loca." His album, titled *Ricky Martin,* was selling very quickly. His concerts were selling out the minute tickets went on sale. For some people, this sudden burst of success would have been hard to handle. Martin knew how to deal with the music business, though. Although the United States was discovering him for the first time, he had been a major star in other countries for years. In fact, show-business fame had been a big part of his childhood.

4   Martin was born in Puerto Rico in 1971. His father was a psychologist, and his mother was a secretary. Neither of them had ever worked in entertainment. That didn't stop Martin. By the time he was six years old, he knew he wanted to be a performer.

5   Martin began his career by making commercials. He appeared in thirty television ads over the next six years. Then when he was 12, he joined Menudo, a wildly popular Latin band for young people. Martin stayed with Menudo for five years. During that time, the band traveled all around the world. Martin got used to living in hotels and sleeping on airplanes. He learned how to handle screaming fans. He spent hours signing autographs and sitting or standing in front of the camera posing for photographs.

6   By the time he was 17, Martin needed a rest. As he put it, "My school has been the hotel room and the lobby has been my playground." His role in Menudo gave him little time for friends or family. He hadn't spent much time with his parents in five years. When his grandmother was ill he wasn't even allowed to take time off to see her. Martin was tired of band managers telling him what to do every minute. He was worn out from **rehearsing** up to 16 hours a day. He wasn't happy with his life in Menudo.

7   "I was tired and confused," he says. "I didn't know if I wanted to be a singer or a carpenter."

8   Martin quit Menudo. Although he knew this was the right thing to do, it was still hard to leave behind the fame. "It was a great shock to leave the band," he admits. "I went from being a somebody who was famous and could have anything I wanted to being a nobody who wasn't recognized by anybody."

## Skill Break
### Using Context
Look at paragraph 5 on this page. Find the word *posing* in the last sentence.

What **clues** in the paragraph can help you find the meaning of *posing*?

From the clues, what do you think *posing* means?

9      Martin returned to Puerto Rico to finish high school. Then in 1991, 19-year-old Martin moved to New York. There he spent months just hanging around, trying to figure out what he wanted for his future. "I was just trying to get my head together," he says.

10      After several months, Martin again felt ready to commit himself to the life of a performer. In 1992 he moved to Mexico City and took a starring role in a television soap opera. The following year he moved to Los Angeles and got a role on the popular U.S. soap opera *General Hospital*. He also began playing one of the lead roles in the hit Broadway musical *Les Misérables*.

11      While he grew as an actor, Martin continued to work on his singing career. He recorded four albums, all of them in Spanish. They were huge hits in Latin America, Asia, and Europe. Together they sold 13 million copies. In 1998 one of Martin's songs was chosen as the **anthem** for the World Cup soccer championship. It was "La Copa de la Vida," the same song he would sing at the 1999 Grammy Awards.

12      Because of his life history, Martin knew how to handle the **surge** in his fame that came after his Grammy performance. He knew that this could have a bad effect on his life. So he worked hard to stay calm and focused.

13      "I **meditate** every morning," he says. Some days he spends hours doing this. Even on his busiest days, he finds time for it. "I just ask people, 'Can I have 20 minutes for myself so I can just breathe?' I turn off the radio and television and just sit there and breathe five seconds in, five seconds out, just to find my center."

**Fun Facts**

▶ Martin's family and close friends call him Kiki.

▶ He does not eat meat.

▶ In 2000 he tried skydiving (jumping out of a plane with a parachute) and loved it.

Ricky Martin reaches out to the audience during a concert.

14    Martin also worked hard not to forget those who were less fortunate and had difficult lives. He especially wanted to help children who were victims of poverty and abuse. He set up the Ricky Martin Foundation to bring aid to needy children around the globe. Martin hated to see children suffer.

15    When the tsunami hit Southeast Asia in 2004, Martin knew he had to help. The huge, unexpected wave of ocean water harmed hundreds of thousands of people. He flew to Thailand to see what he could do. "After looking at those images on television, it was impossible for me to stay at home with my arms crossed," he said. He arranged to have his foundation help rebuild homes in the area.

16    Someone asked Martin if he planned to perform while in Thailand. He answered, "I don't think this time is about performing. It's about understanding the needs of this town and creating a plan so that we can really do something."

17    For Ricky Martin, being a star was great. But he had learned early in life that fame comes and goes. So he focused on helping others and on "enjoying life as it comes." As he said, "We know about today. We don't know about tomorrow."

# A  Understanding What You Read

◆ Fill in the circle next to the correct answer.

**1.** Which of the following statements is an opinion rather than a fact?

○ A. Millions of TV viewers tuned in to watch.
○ B. The awards show had been pretty dull.
○ C. The song lasted 210 seconds.

**2.** Before he performed at the 1999 Grammy Awards, Martin had

○ A. never been on TV before.
○ B. been a member of a Latin band.
○ C. played championship soccer.

**3.** What caused Martin to leave the group Menudo?

○ A. He wanted to help people in Asia.
○ B. He got a starring role in a soap opera.
○ C. He needed a rest from the travel and work.

**4.** Ricky Martin went to Thailand in 2004 to

○ A. perform a concert for his fans.
○ B. record a new Spanish album.
○ C. create a plan to rebuild homes.

**5.** How is Ricky Martin an example of a generous person?

○ A. He gives aid to needy children around the world.
○ B. He works hard to stay calm and focused every day.
○ C. He has been singing and acting since he was a child.

_____ Number of Correct Answers: Part A

# B  Using Context

◆ Read the paragraph below. Look for context clues that tell you what the phrase *less fortunate* means. Underline at least **two** context clues in the paragraph. Then fill in the circle next to the correct meaning of *less fortunate*.

**1.**

Martin also worked hard not to forget those who were <u>less fortunate</u> and had difficult lives. He especially wanted to help children who were victims of poverty and abuse. He set up the Ricky Martin Foundation to bring aid to needy children around the globe. Martin hated to see children suffer.

○ A. not wealthy or not in a good situation
○ B. not wanting to leave their homes
○ C. not needing any help or assistance

◆ Reread paragraph 15 in the article. Find the word *tsunami* near the beginning of the paragraph. Look for context clues about the meaning of *tsunami*. Write the clues on the lines below. Then write what you think *tsunami* means.

**2.** Context Clues: _____

_____

*Tsunami* means: _____

_____

# C Using Words

◆ Complete each sentence with a word from the box. Write the missing word on the line.

| | | |
|---|---|---|
| electrified | anthem | meditate |
| rehearsing | surge | |

**1.** She always feels more relaxed after she takes time to

_____.

**2.** I felt a _____ of energy after I ate that apple.

**3.** He started _____ the song two weeks before the performance.

**4.** We sing the national _____ at the beginning of every baseball game.

**5.** The sports fans were _____ when their team scored the winning point.

◆ Choose one word from the box. Write a new sentence using the word.

**6.** word: _____

_____

_____ Number of Correct Answers: Part C

## D | Writing About It

### Write a Postcard

◆ Write a postcard to Ricky Martin. Finish the sentences below to write your postcard. Use the checklist on page 103 to check your work.

Dear Mr. Martin,

I just read an article about you. I liked reading

about_____

_____.

I think you _____

_____.

I was wondering_____

_____.

Sincerely,

_____

Mr. Ricky Martin
345 Martin Ln.
Rickytown, USA

**Lesson 1** Add your correct answers from parts A, B, and C to get your total score. Then find the percentage for your total score on the chart below. Record your percentage on the graph on page 105.

_____ Total Score for Parts A, B, and C

_____ Percentage

| Total Score | 1 | 2 | 3 | 4 | 5 | 6 | 7 | 8 | 9 | 10 | 11 | 12 | 13 |
|---|---|---|---|---|---|---|---|---|---|---|---|---|---|
| Percentage | 8 | 15 | 23 | 31 | 38 | 46 | 54 | 62 | 69 | 77 | 85 | 92 | 100 |

# Ellen MacArthur
## Sailing Around the World

**Birth Name** Ellen Patricia MacArthur

**Birth Date and Place** July 8, 1976; Whatstandwell, Derbyshire, England

**Home** Cowes, Isle of Wight, UK

# Think About What You Know

Have you ever had to do something really difficult all by yourself? How did you do it? Read the article and find out about Ellen MacArthur's difficult sailing trip.

# Word Power

What do the words below tell you about the article?

**unattended** not watched or not taken care of

**hull** the outer frame of a ship

**generator** a machine that creates electricity

**collision** two things crashing into one another

**landlocked** completely surrounded by land with no large bodies of water nearby

# Reading Skill

**Cause and Effect** Many stories and articles show cause and effect. A **cause** tells *why* something happened. An **effect** tells *what* happened. The cause happens first. Then, as a result, the effect happens. The word *because* can help you find the cause. The words *so* and *as a result* can help you find the effect. You can also find the cause by asking *why* something happened.

| Example | |
|---|---|
| **Cause** | Because my dad took a sailing class when he was a |
| **Effect** | child, he thinks he is an expert on sailing. |

The effect in the paragraph is "He thinks he is an expert on sailing." The cause is "My dad took a sailing class when he was a child." To find the cause, you can ask yourself *why*. When you answer the question *why*, the words that come after the word *because* show the cause. *Why* does he think he is an expert on sailing?

# Ellen MacArthur

## Sailing Around the World

Ellen MacArthur felt nervous. She had been at sea less than two weeks, but already things were going wrong. MacArthur had left England on November 28, 2004. She was alone in her 75-foot boat, named the *B&Q.* Her plan was to sail all the way around the world. She hoped to beat the world-record time set by Francis Joyon a few months earlier. Joyon had made the trip in just less than 73 days. MacArthur thought she could do it faster. After only 13 days of her journey, though, she was close to giving up.

2   It had been a hard trip from the start. Because it wasn't safe to leave the boat **unattended** for more than 20 or 30 minutes, MacArthur got very little sleep. There was always a great deal to do. She had to watch the wind closely. As the wind changed, she had to change her sails. Each change took 30 to 40 minutes. Sometimes she had to make 15 changes a day. This wasn't her only challenge, either.

3   On Day 4, MacArthur's fresh-water tank started leaking. By Day 9, she was covered with sores from the constant spray of salt water on her body. On Day 15, the wind and the waves got very rough. She wrote, "Everything is flying around the cabin. I have to hold on to something the whole time to stop being flung across the boat. I've had my head smashed against the **hull** a few times."

4   On Day 13, MacArthur hit a new low. Her **generator** wasn't working correctly. Heat and fumes were filling the cabin. "I got to the stage where I couldn't breathe in the boat," she wrote. For three days, MacArthur struggled to solve the problem. "I was absolutely at my wits' end." She knew that if she couldn't fix the problem she would have to admit defeat and sail sadly back home to England.

5    Luckily, by Day 17, MacArthur got the generator fixed. Just a few days later, she had more trouble. Another fierce storm hammered the ship. This one lasted three days. "I am getting launched sideways," she wrote. "I am literally gripping on to the chart table with my fingernails." At one point during the storm, the *B&Q* hit a large fish. MacArthur feared the **collision** had damaged the ship, but it hadn't. "I was very, very lucky," she wrote.

6    Day 28 was Christmas Day. MacArthur wasn't even halfway through the trip, but the stress was affecting her badly. She was so tired she could barely think. She had a terrible headache. Even her tongue had sores on it from the salt and the stress. To make matters worse, the weather was still awful. "Right now we are in the center of a storm," she wrote, talking about her and her boat. "The only white Christmas is the breaking waves all around us."

7    This sailing journey was so difficult that some people wonder why MacArthur tried to do it at all. The answer is that she had wanted to go to sea ever since she was a child. She grew up in the **landlocked** town of Derbyshire, England. Although she didn't have much experience with the ocean, she dreamed of owning her own boat. After finishing school, she worked her way up through the sailing world until she was quite well known. By age 25, she felt ready for one of the greatest challenges of sailing. She would try to sail alone around the world.

## Skill Break
### Cause and Effect

Look at paragraph 7 on this page. This paragraph shows cause and effect, but clue words do not appear here. You can ask questions to help you find the cause and the effect. The **effect** is that MacArthur went on a difficult sailing journey. What is the **cause?**

What **question** could you ask to help you find the cause?

8    MacArthur set out on that trip in November of 2000 and managed to complete the journey in 94 days. She was the youngest person who had ever done the trip. Even though 94 days was also the fastest any woman had done it, that still wasn't enough for MacArthur. She wanted to push herself harder. She wanted to set the all-time speed record for the journey.

9    Now here she was, 350 miles south of New Zealand, surrounded by icebergs and battered by terrible storms. On January 4, 2005, she wrote, "I'm totally exhausted. I have never sailed in conditions like this before—not for this long." The next day she added, "My body has been pushed beyond its limits."

10   It might have seemed that things couldn't get any worse. But they could, and they did. On Day 39, MacArthur burned her arm on the generator. "It was so bad I took my shirt off straight away to check it and it had immediately blistered," she wrote. Ten days later, during another bad storm, one of the sails swung around and hit her in the head. "Blood everywhere," she wrote.

11   Perhaps the worst moment of all came on Day 55. The *B&Q*'s main sail broke loose. To fix it, MacArthur had to climb to the top of the mast. As she scrambled up the 90-foot pole, giant waves rocked the boat. One person whom she had sailed with back in England imagined that this must have been like "hanging on to a telegraph pole in an earthquake."

**Fun Facts**

▶ Before her trip, MacArthur worked with a sleep expert to learn how to get through the day with very little sleep.

▶ She wrote two books about her sailing adventures called *Taking on the World* and *Race Against Time*.

Ellen MacArthur broke a world record by sailing around the world in less than 72 days.

12    By the time MacArthur had climbed down, her whole body was badly bruised. "Every muscle in my body feels like it's been torn," she wrote. "I've got massive bruises on my left leg from where it was jammed between the sail and the mast." She still felt pleased with her effort. "I'm pretty happy to have managed to repair the mast," she noted.

13    Over the next 15 days, MacArthur had more problems. She was behind schedule. Her boat nearly hit a whale. She had to endure more horrible storms. However, on February 7, 2005, MacArthur finally made it back to England. Her time was 71 days, 14 hours, 18 minutes, and 33 seconds. She had done it! She had beaten Joyon's record by about 32 hours.

14    "This trip has taken pretty much ALL I have, every last drop and ounce," she admitted. "It's been an absolutely unbelievable journey, both physically and mentally." Despite the pain, her trip had been rewarding. When she stepped off the boat onto dry land and into the record books, MacArthur's tears were tears of joy.

# A Understanding What You Read

◆ **Fill in the circle next to the correct answer.**

**1.** During MacArthur's trip, the constant spray of salt water

○ A. caused things to fly around MacArthur's cabin.

○ B. made it very hard for MacArthur to sleep.

○ C. created sores all over MacArthur's body.

**2.** MacArthur spent Christmas of 2004

○ A. with her family in Derbyshire.

○ B. in the center of an awful storm.

○ C. trying to repair the ship's generator.

**3.** From what the article told you about sailing, you can conclude that

○ A. few people have sailed around the world alone.

○ B. it's easier to sail alone than to sail with others.

○ C. stormy weather always makes a ship sail faster.

**4.** From the information in the article, you can predict that MacArthur will

○ A. team up with Francis Joyon for her next race.

○ B. sell her sailboat and buy a bigger one.

○ C. take time to rest before starting another trip.

**5.** Which sentence **best** states the main idea of the article?

○ A. MacArthur is a brave sailor who set a world record.

○ B. MacArthur is a famous woman from England.

○ C. MacArthur is strong enough to fix a broken sail.

_____ Number of Correct Answers: Part A

## B  Understanding Cause and Effect

◆ Read the paragraph below. The paragraph shows cause and effect. The effect is that MacArthur got very little sleep. Fill in the circle next to the sentence that shows the **cause.**

**1.**

It had been a hard trip right from the start. Because it wasn't safe to leave the boat unattended for more than 20 or 30 minutes, MacArthur got very little sleep. There was always a great deal to do. She had to watch the wind closely. As the wind changed, she had to change her sails. Each change took 30 to 40 minutes. Sometimes she had to make 15 changes a day. This wasn't her only challenge, either.

○ A. Each sail change took 30 to 40 minutes.
○ B. It wasn't safe to leave the boat unattended for long.
○ C. Changing the sails often was only one of her challenges.

◆ Reread paragraph 4 in the article. The paragraph shows cause and effect. The effect is that MacArthur couldn't breathe in the boat. What question can you ask to find the **cause?** Write the question and the cause on the lines below.

**2.** Question: _____

_____

Cause: _____

_____

_____ Number of Correct Answers: Part B

# C Using Words

◆ Cross out one of the four words in each row that does **not** relate to the word in dark type.

**1. unattended**

ignore                gone                copy                deserted

**2. hull**

cliff                ship                outside                body

**3. generator**

engine                power                words                motor

**4. collision**

accident                broken                hit                asleep

**5. landlocked**

water                wind                dry                earth

◆ Choose one of the words shown in dark type above. Write a sentence using the word.

**6.** word: _____

_____

_____

_____ Number of Correct Answers: Part C

## D  Writing About It

### Write a Journal Entry

◆ Suppose you had seen Ellen MacArthur arrive in England on February 7, 2005. Write a journal entry about what you saw and thought. Finish the sentences below to write your journal entry. Use the checklist on page 103 to check your work.

February 7, 2005

Today I saw Ellen MacArthur finish her trip around the world. I wanted to see her boat arrive because _____

_____.

When she stepped off the boat, _____

_____.

I wonder if _____

_____.

**Lesson 2**  Add your correct answers from parts A, B, and C to get your total score. Then find the percentage for your total score on the chart below. Record your percentage on the graph on page 105.

_____ Total Score for Parts A, B, and C

_____ Percentage

| Total Score | 1 | 2 | 3 | 4 | 5 | 6 | 7 | 8 | 9 | 10 | 11 | 12 | 13 |
|---|---|---|---|---|---|---|---|---|---|---|---|---|---|
| Percentage | 8 | 15 | 23 | 31 | 38 | 46 | 54 | 62 | 69 | 77 | 85 | 92 | 100 |

# Bethany Hamilton
## Living Through a Shark Attack

**Birth Name** Bethany Hamilton

**Birth Date and Place** February 8, 1990; North Shore, Kaua'i, Hawaii

**Home** Princeville, Kaua'i, Hawaii

# Think About What You Know

Have you ever seen a movie or read a book about sharks? What do you know about people who have been bitten by sharks? Read the article and find out how Bethany Hamilton survived a shark attack.

# Word Power

What do the words below tell you about the article?

**lurked** moved around while staying hidden from view

**conscious** awake and aware

**shell-shocked** upset because of a sudden, terrible event

**deadline** a time or date when something must be finished

**carefree** without worries

# Reading Skill

**Making Predictions** A **prediction** is a good guess about what will happen later in a story or article. Good readers make predictions based on clues from the text and what they already know. Good readers change their predictions as they read more of the story or article.

**Example**

One week before my brother's swimming test, he broke his arm. The doctor put a cast on his arm to help it heal. My brother would have to wear the cast for at least a month. The doctor said the cast would need to be kept clean and dry.

From the information in the paragraph, you can predict that *the author's brother will not be able to take his swimming test.* One clue to make this prediction is "The doctor said the cast would need to be kept clean and dry." What other clues tell you that the brother will not be able to take the swimming test? How does what you already know help you use these clues?

23

# Bethany Hamilton
## Living Through a Shark Attack

**O**ctober 21, 2003, began like an ordinary day. Thirteen-year-old Bethany Hamilton got up about 5:00 A.M., as usual. By the time the sun rose, she and her friend Alana Blanchard were out on their surfboards. They were two of the best young surfers in the United States. They loved catching waves off the beaches of the Hawaiian island of Kaua'i.

2    On this day, they had chosen Makua Beach. The sea offered clear blue water and gentle waves. Though it looked like a perfect day for the young surfers, a terrible danger **lurked** beneath the surface of the water. That danger was a 15-foot tiger shark.

3    Around 7:30 A.M., Hamilton took a break from her workout. She didn't return to shore, though. Instead she rested on her surfboard with her left hand hanging in the water. Alana Blanchard and her father, Holt Blanchard, were nearby.

4    Without warning, the shark attacked. "All I saw was a grey blur," recalls Hamilton. The shark came up through the water, opened its huge jaws, and clamped down hard. It bit a large chunk out of Hamilton's surfboard. With the same bite, it took off Hamilton's left arm just a few inches from her shoulder. "My arm went straight down the shark's throat," she says. The shark shook its head to be sure it had cut loose a mouthful. Then it disappeared under the waves.

5    Hamilton was stunned. "I watched in shock as the water around me turned red," she says. After a moment, she realized it was her own blood that was coloring the water. That's when she called to Alana and Holt Blanchard.

6    "I got attacked by a shark," she said in a surprisingly calm voice.

7  Hamilton was able to paddle to Holt Blanchard. With her remaining arm, she grabbed his leg and hung on as he frantically swam the quarter mile back to shore. Once on land, Holt grabbed a rubber leash from a surfboard. He tied it tightly around what remained of Hamilton's arm to slow the flow of blood from her body. By the time rescue workers got her to the hospital, she was barely **conscious.** She had lost more than half her blood.

8  "You've lost your arm," a doctor told her. "Now the focus is on saving your life."

9  Hamilton had two operations over the next three days. She survived, but only four inches of her left arm remained. That left some big questions. Were her surfing days over? Would she ever have the balance and strength to stand on a surfboard again?

10  "Imagine the one thing you love to do the most," says Hamilton. "Now imagine something happens and you may never be able to do it again. How do you feel? Sad? Angry? **Shell-shocked?** For me, the answer was all of the above."

11  Hamilton vowed to do whatever it took to return to surfing. Before the attack, she had been ranked eighth in the world among amateur surfboarders. She was determined to return to that level and even go beyond it. "My goal has always been, and still is, to surf competitively," she said.

## Skill Break
### Making Predictions

Think about what you have read so far. Using clues in the text, what do you think is most likely to **happen next?**

What **clues** did you use to make your prediction?

How did **what you already** know help you use the clues?

As you read the rest of the article, check to see if what happens next matches your prediction.

12    Hamilton set a **deadline** for herself. She wanted to be back on a surfboard by Thanksgiving. That was just four weeks away. She immediately started building up her strength. She had to learn to do everything one-handed, from getting dressed to opening bottles. Some of these things were difficult, but surfing would be especially hard. Hamilton's entire sense of balance had been thrown off. "Paddling and surfing with one arm requires complete changes," she said. Still, she insisted she could do it.

13    The day before Thanksgiving, Hamilton felt ready to go back in the water. She and her family went to the beach. Bravely, Hamilton began paddling away from shore. Then for the first time since the shark attack, she tried to stand up on her surfboard. "My first couple of tries I couldn't get up," she says. "Then it happened. A wave rolled through, I caught it, put my hand on the deck to push up and I was standing. Everyone was cheering. It was a great moment!"

14    After that there was no stopping Hamilton. Just 10 weeks after the attack, she was competing again. She finished fifth in a National Scholastic Surfing Association (NSSA) meet. Officials had offered to give her extra time between performances, but Hamilton refused. As one official explained, "She said she wanted to be treated like anybody else." Hamilton didn't feel sorry for herself and she didn't want others to feel sorry for her, either.

**Fun Facts**

▶ Hamilton started surfing at age five and competing at age eight.

▶ She also likes other sports, such as snowboarding and horseback riding.

▶ She has a horse named Coco.

Bethany Hamilton surfs in a contest against Hawaii's best young surfers.

15  The doctors had made an artificial arm for Hamilton. She was grateful, but she did not want the arm. She knew it was supposed to make her look more "normal," but she had accepted the fact that she had only one arm. She believed others could learn to accept it too. "I think I look fine," she said. So her artificial arm stays packed away in her closet.

16  Hamilton's courage has touched everyone's heart. She now has fans all around the world. Hamilton has used her fame to help others. She has visited U.S. soldiers injured in Iraq. She has raised money for victims of the tsunami that struck Asia in 2004. Hamilton has also written a book. It is called *Soul Surfer: A True Story of Faith, Family, and Fighting to Get Back on the Board.* In 2005 she began working on a movie about her life.

17  Of course, Hamilton also continues to surf. In 2005 she placed first in the Explorer Women's division of NSSA's national championships. She admits that she is not quite as **carefree** in the water as she used to be. Sometimes she gets scared when she sees shadows in the water. "I think about sharks all the time," she says. She won't let fear rule her life, though. She says, "To stop something you love so much is like stopping your life."

# A  Understanding What You Read

◆ Fill in the circle next to the correct answer or write the answer.

**1.** From what you read in the article, which of these is probably true?

○ A. Makua Beach is on the Hawaiian island of Maui.

○ B. Alana Blanchard is much older than Hamilton.

○ C. The shark attack on Hamilton happened quickly.

**2.** Choose from the letters below to correctly complete the following statement. Write the letters on the lines.

On the bad side, _____, but on the good side, _____.

A. Hamilton got up at 5:00 A.M.

B. Hamilton lost her arm

C. Hamilton survived the attack

**3.** Before Hamilton tried surfing again, she had to

○ A. write a book about her life.

○ B. build strength and find her balance.

○ C. take extra time between performances.

**4.** Hamilton did not want an artificial arm because

○ A. she thought she looked fine without it.

○ B. she had packed it away in her closet.

○ C. she found it very difficult to use.

**5.** In which paragraph did you find the information to answer question 4?

_____

_____ Number of Correct Answers: Part A

28

**Making Predictions**

◆ Read the paragraph below. Look at the clues in the paragraph. Fill in the circle next to the prediction that is **most likely** to happen based on the clues.

**1.**

   Hamilton set a deadline for herself. She wanted to be back on a surfboard by Thanksgiving. That was just four weeks away. She immediately started building up her strength. She had to learn to do everything one-handed, from getting dressed to opening bottles. Some of these things were difficult, but surfing would be especially hard. Hamilton's entire sense of balance had been thrown off. "Paddling and surfing with one arm requires complete changes," she said. Still, she insisted she could do it.

   ○ A. Hamilton will become a professional weight lifter.
   ○ B. Hamilton will be surfing again before her deadline.
   ○ C. Hamilton's family will not let her go back in the water.

◆ What clues in the paragraph helped you make the prediction? How did what you already know help you make the prediction? Write **two** clues and what you already know on the lines.

**2.** Clues: _____

_____

What I Know: _____

_____

_____ Number of Correct Answers: Part B

## C   Using Words

◆ The words and phrases in the list below relate to the words in the box. Some words or phrases in the list have a meaning that is the same as or similar to a word in the box. Some have the opposite meaning. Write the related word from the box on each line. Use each word from the box twice.

| | | |
|---|---|---|
| lurked | shell-shocked | carefree |
| conscious | deadline | |

**Same or similar meaning**

1. relaxed _____

2. end date _____

3. sneaked _____

4. distressed _____

5. alert _____

6. time limit _____

**Opposite meaning**

7. asleep _____

8. came into view _____

9. concerned _____

10. calm _____

_____ Number of Correct Answers: Part C

**Writing About It**

## Write Your Thoughts

◆ Finish the sentence below. Use the checklist on page 103 to check your work.

I can't believe _____

_____.

## How Did You Do?

◆ Finish the sentence below. Use the checklist on page 103 to check your work.

When reading the article, I was having trouble with _____

_____

_____.

---

**Lesson 3** Add your correct answers from parts A, B, and C to get your total score. Then find the percentage for your total score on the chart below. Record your percentage on the graph on page 105.

_____ Total Score for Parts A, B, and C

_____ Percentage

| Total Score | 1 | 2 | 3 | 4 | 5 | 6 | 7 | 8 | 9 | 10 | 11 | 12 | 13 | 14 | 15 | 16 | 17 |
|---|---|---|---|---|---|---|---|---|---|---|---|---|---|---|---|---|---|
| Percentage | 6 | 12 | 18 | 24 | 29 | 35 | 41 | 47 | 53 | 59 | 65 | 71 | 76 | 82 | 88 | 94 | 100 |

# Compare and Contrast

 Think about the celebrities, or famous people, in Unit One. Pick two articles that tell about celebrities who needed their bodies to be strong to reach a goal. Use information from the articles to fill in this chart.

| Celebrity's Name | | |
|---|---|---|
| What was the celebrity's goal? | | |
| What happened to the celebrity's body that created a challenge? | | |
| How did the celebrity get past this challenge and reach the goal? | | |

LeBron James

Adam Beach

Jet Li

# LeBron James

## Great From the Start

**Birth Name** LeBron James

**Birth Date and Place** December 30, 1984; Akron, Ohio

**Home** Cleveland, Ohio

# Think About What You Know

What are your strongest talents? Which ones did you work hard to develop? Which ones came naturally to you? Read the article and find out about LeBron James and his talent for playing basketball.

# Word Power

What do the words below tell you about the article?

**observer** a person who is watching something carefully

**miniature** very small

**phenomenal** extraordinary or fantastic

**ego** pride or confidence in oneself

**typical** a good example of something

# Reading Skill

**Using Context** **Context clues** can help you find the meaning of a word that you don't understand. Context clues are other words in the same sentence or in nearby sentences. If you don't understand a word, look for clues around it that might help you. Then try to find the meaning.

**Example**

**Context Clues**

**New Word**

Our school basketball team has been having a great season. We were really looking forward to our game last night. Then we discovered that our best player was sick and couldn't play. Our team played terribly without him. The game was a rout. We lost by 30 points.

If you don't know the meaning of the word *rout,* you can use the context clues "Our team played terribly" and "We lost by 30 points" to help you find the meaning. From these clues, what do you think *rout* means?

# LeBron James
## Great From the Start

The coaches could see it coming. The tall skinny kid was going to be a star. It wasn't just LeBron James's height that made him stick out—although he was several inches taller than his teammates. What really separated James from everyone else was the way he played basketball.

2   When James was on the court, he seemed able to do anything. He was quick and strong. He could grab rebounds, make passes, and set up his own shots. One **observer** said it was like James had a coach inside his head telling him what to do. James himself said, "It's like I see things before they happen. I kind of know where the defenders are [going to] be. I kind of know where my teammates are [going to] be, sometimes even before they know."

3   James's talent emerged at an early age. It first came out when he was a small child. He showed great interest in basketball, and when his mother gave him a **miniature** ball and hoop, he played with them for hours. That wasn't unusual. Many small children play with balls. But when James got old enough to play basketball for real, his ability stood out. It was clear that he was someone special. When he was just eight years old, a coach asked him to help instruct, or teach, the other kids.

4   By the time James was 10, he had joined an Amateur Athletic Union (AAU) team called the Shooting Stars. This team traveled around the country playing against other AAU teams. When James was 12, the Shooting Stars made it to the national championship. Even on this elite, high-ranking team, James was a leader. He could easily play all five positions. "You could tell he was a basketball genius," says one of the coaches.

5    When James was old enough for high school, many schools wanted him for their teams. James chose a school in Akron, Ohio, St. Vincent-St. Mary's. Many people had high hopes for James, and he didn't disappoint. In his freshman year, he averaged just under 20 points per game. He helped "St. V's" win its first state championship in many years. Over the next three years, James got bigger and better.

6    The summer after his freshman year, James grew almost 4 inches. This put him at 6 feet 7 inches tall. As a sophomore he averaged 25 points, 7 rebounds, 5 assists, and 4 steals. By the time he was a senior, he had grown another inch and began to outshine most of his teammates and opponents. The players at St. V's had averages that were the best in the league, but James's averages were still better. His scoring average was up near 30 points, and he was averaging 13 rebounds per game.

7    By then the entire country was watching this **phenomenal** young player. James's games brought in many more people than the average high-school basketball game did. They drew so many fans that his school had to rent a 5,000-seat arena! Many of his games were shown on television. National Basketball Association (NBA) players started noticing him too. The legendary Michael Jordan invited James to some private practice sessions. There, James got to play with other well-known NBA stars such as Antoine Walker, Juwan Howard, and Michael Finley. When James turned 18, another famous player, Allen Iverson, called to wish him a happy birthday.

## Skill Break
### Using Context
Look at paragraph 6 on this page. Find the word *outshine* in the middle of the paragraph.

What **clues** in the paragraph can help you find the meaning of *outshine*?
From the clues, what do you think *outshine* means?

8    Faced with this kind of attention, most teenagers would have had trouble keeping their **ego** under control. James was able to stay humble, though. He had learned that basketball is the most fun when it is played as a team sport. In other words, it's not about one player doing well. James certainly could dominate the court, but he seemed just as happy being a leader by passing the ball to teammates, setting them up to make great plays, and playing tight defense.

9    The unselfish way that James plays had been encouraged by his childhood coaches, and James has stayed focused on teamwork throughout his career so far. Again and again, he includes his teammates in his success. The comment James made after a 2002 high-school game is **typical** of his leadership style and attitude, or way of being. "Tonight I was looking to pass and get my teammates into it," he said. That same season he told a reporter, "I only want to make my teammates better." As *Sports Illustrated* writer Jack McCallum said, James "could have averaged 50 points but settled for a modest 30."

10   Given his talent, it was no surprise that James chose to go straight to the NBA after high school. He was already a better player than many professionals. Besides, during his high-profile years in high school, James had gotten used to having a lot of public attention. "I've been going through it for two years," he said. "I can handle it."

**Fun Facts**

▶ James made his first slam dunk when he was 14 years old.

▶ His nickname is King James.
▶ He really likes football and was a star player on his high-school football team.

LeBron James gets ready to shoot a free throw during an NBA game.

11    Many people agreed that James was ready for the NBA. Said former Celtics star Danny Ainge, "I think he's the best high school player I've seen in my life. I've seen Magic [Johnson], Gene Banks, Jonathan Bender, Tracy McGrady, Lamar Odom, and Kobe Bryant. He's better than all of those guys."

12    However, some people wondered if being 18 years old and going straight into the NBA from high school would be too hard. They didn't have to worry. James fit right in. During his first season, he helped the Cleveland Cavaliers double their number of wins. James averaged 21 points, 6 assists, and 5 rebounds. At the same time, he remained a team player. During his first season with the Cavaliers, he said, "If there's one message I want to get to my teammates it's that I'll be there for them, do whatever they think I need to do."

13    By 2005 James had become the youngest NBA player to reach 2,000 career points, 500 assists, and 500 rebounds. After just two seasons, he was one of the most promising players in the league. While no one can predict the future, it seems safe to say that LeBron James will be a major force in the NBA for years to come.

# A Understanding What You Read

◆ **Fill in the circle next to the correct answer.**

**1.** When he was eight years old, a coach asked James to

  ○ A. play on an AAU team.
  ○ B. help teach other kids.
  ○ C. work on his passing.

**2.** What was the effect of James joining the AAU Shooting Stars?

  ○ A. James led the team to the championships.
  ○ B. James was noticed by famous NBA players.
  ○ C. *Sports Illustrated* wrote an article about James.

**3.** James learned that he enjoys basketball most when he

  ○ A. scores more than 30 points.
  ○ B. plays it like a team sport.
  ○ C. gets a lot of attention.

**4.** From the information in the article, you can predict that James will

  ○ A. have trouble keeping his pride under control.
  ○ B. start shooting more and passing the ball less.
  ○ C. always be well-respected by his teammates.

**5.** Which sentence **best** states the lesson about life that this article teaches?

  ○ A. Good leaders focus on supporting their team.
  ○ B. What other people think of you is not important.
  ○ C. Don't put all of your energy into one activity.

_____ Number of Correct Answers: Part A

## B  Using Context

◆ Read the paragraph below. Look for context clues that tell you what the word *drew* means. Underline **at least two** context clues in the paragraph. Then fill in the circle next to the correct meaning of *drew*.

**1.**

By then, the entire country was watching this phenomenal young player. James's games brought in many more people than the average high-school basketball game did. They <u>drew</u> so many fans that his school had to rent a 5,000-seat arena! Many of his games were shown on television. National Basketball Association (NBA) players started noticing him too. The legendary Michael Jordan invited James to some private practice sessions. There, James got to play with other well-known NBA stars such as Antoine Walker, Juwan Howard, and Michael Finley. When James turned 18, another famous player, Allen Iverson, called to wish him a happy birthday.

○ A. marked onto paper
○ B. caused to come
○ C. thought about

◆ Reread paragraph 10 in the article. Find the phrase *high-profile* in the middle of the paragraph. Look for a context clue about the meaning of *high-profile*. Write **one** clue on the lines below. Then write what you think *high-profile* means.

**2.** Context Clue: _____

*High-profile* means: _____

_____ Number of Correct Answers: Part B

# C Using Words

◆ Cross out one of the four words in each row that does **not** relate to the word in dark type.

**1. observer**

| see | notice | attention | speed |

**2. miniature**

| tiny | smart | little | shrink |

**3. phenomenal**

| amaze | dry | rare | unusual |

**4. ego**

| easy | proud | self | person |

**5. typical**

| normal | expected | hope | usual |

◆ Choose one of the words shown in dark type above. Write a sentence using the word.

**6.** word: _____

_____

_____

_____ Number of Correct Answers: Part C

42

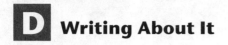

## **D** Writing About It

### Write a Poem

◆ Write a poem about LeBron James playing basketball. Finish the sentences below to write your poem. Use the checklist on page 103 to check your work.

### Watching LeBron James

Watching LeBron James play is like watching _____.

He always keeps _____.

On the basketball court, his moves _____.

If he were an animal, he would be _____.

**Lesson 4** Add your correct answers from parts A, B, and C to get your total score. Then find the percentage for your total score on the chart below. Record your percentage on the graph on page 105.

_____ Total Score for Parts A, B, and C

_____ Percentage

| Total Score | 1 | 2 | 3 | 4 | 5 | 6 | 7 | 8 | 9 | 10 | 11 | 12 | 13 |
|---|---|---|---|---|---|---|---|---|---|---|---|---|---|
| Percentage | 8 | 15 | 23 | 31 | 38 | 46 | 54 | 62 | 69 | 77 | 85 | 92 | 100 |

# Adam Beach

## Faithful to His Roots

**Birth Name** Adam Ruebin Beach

**Birth Date and Place** November 11, 1972; Ashern, Manitoba, Canada

**Home** Los Angeles, California

# Think About What You Know

Where did your ancestors come from? What kind of culture did they have? How do your roots affect your life today? Read the article and find out about Adam Beach and his Native American roots.

# Word Power

What do the words below tell you about the article?

**aboriginal** one of the first, or original, groups of people to live in an area

**stereotyped** treated as if everyone in a certain group is exactly alike

**bitter** full of disappointment and bad feelings

**disapproved** did not like or did not support what someone was doing

**complex** difficult to understand

# Reading Skill

**Cause and Effect** Many stories and articles show cause and effect. A **cause** tells *why* something happened. An **effect** tells *what* happened. The cause happens first. Then, as a result, the effect happens. You can ask the question *Why did this happen?* to find the cause. Ask *What happened as a result?* to find the effect.

| Example | |
|---|---|
| **Cause** | The young boy loved performing in school plays. |
| **Effect** | When he went to college, he chose to study drama. |

The cause in the paragraph is "While growing up, the boy loved performing in school plays." The effect is "When he went to college, he chose to study drama." To find the cause you can ask, *Why did he choose to study drama?* What question can you ask to find the effect?

# Adam Beach

## Faithful to His Roots

"I am proud of who I am."

2  That's what Adam Beach says when people ask him about his choice of movie roles. During his 15-year acting career, Beach has made a point of only playing Native American characters. Sometimes a character's heritage is an important part of the movie, and sometimes it isn't. Beach has never taken a role that required him to turn his back on his own roots, though.

3  "I am Indian," he says. "I am Saulteaux. I'm native. I am **aboriginal,** whatever word they have. That's who I am and I'm not letting anybody use that in a negative way. When people say, 'Adam, do you feel you're **stereotyped** in film?' I say, 'No, because I am Indian. I am proud of who I am.'"

4  Choosing to play only Native American characters may have limited Beach's film opportunities, but that's a price he is willing to pay. He is happy with his life choices—so happy, in fact, that in one recent film, the director told Beach that he had to quit smiling so much. Beach has not always been so content, though.

5  Beach was born on the Dog Creek Indian Reserve in Manitoba, Canada. When he was seven years old, two terrible accidents changed his life forever. First his mother was killed by a drunk driver. Then, just two months later, his father drowned. Suddenly Beach and his two younger brothers found themselves orphaned. Against their wishes, the boys were sent to Winnipeg to stay with an aunt and uncle. The boys had never lived in a city before. So in addition to dealing with the pain of their parents' deaths, the boys also had to adjust to city life. Five years later, they moved again to live with a different aunt and uncle.

6　　The experience of losing his parents made Beach angry and **bitter.** He tried to take care of his younger brothers, but it was difficult because he was struggling with his own grief at the same time. In Winnipeg he attended a school with mostly white students. This added to Beach's feeling that he didn't really belong anywhere. At age 12, he joined a street gang and made some bad choices. He says he "didn't want to be a part of anything. I'd steal clothes. My friends needed jeans and I would get them." Later he tried playing in a band, but it didn't last long.

7　　In 10th grade, Beach decided to sign up for a drama class. He wasn't serious about acting. He simply thought the class would give him a chance to be with his friends. To his surprise, Beach discovered that he had a natural talent for acting. On stage he was free to show all of his emotions. "I began to express myself in a safe way," he says.

8　　Beach got an added boost by watching Johnny Depp on the TV show *21 Jump Street*. Depp is part Cherokee. Beach thought that if Depp could be a professional actor, then maybe he could be one too.

9　　At age 16, Beach joined a local theater company and soon got his first professional part. It was a very small role in the 1990 TV movie *Lost in the Barrens*. After that, Beach got a part in another TV movie called *Spirit Rider*. "I played an angry kid, and I was good at that," says Beach.

## Skill Break

### Cause and Effect

Look at paragraph 7 on this page. This paragraph shows cause and effect. The **cause** is that Beach decided to sign up for a drama class. What is the **effect?**

What **question** could you ask to help you find the effect?

10    By this time, Beach knew he wanted to make acting his career. His friends and family thought he was crazy. "Every, every, every, every, every, everyone said, 'When are you [going to] quit and get a real job?'" he recalls.

11    Although many people **disapproved**, Beach kept acting. In 1994 he starred in a Disney film called *Squanto: A Warrior's Tale.* Other projects followed. In 1998 he starred in *Smoke Signals,* a movie that won awards at the Sundance Film Festival. The next year he appeared with Russell Crowe in the movie *Mystery, Alaska.* Then in 2002, he was given a starring role alongside Nicholas Cage in the movie *Windtalkers.*

12    *Windtalkers* is based on the true story of work done by Navajo people during World War II. Leaders in the United States were looking for a code that the Japanese could not break. They went to the Navajo for help. Navajo soldiers became "code talkers," sending messages in their native language. The Navajo language is so **complex** that the Japanese never did figure out the code.

13    John Woo, the film's director, hoped to use a Navajo actor to play the part of code talker Ben Yahzee. But as Woo recalls, "It was difficult to find real Navajos who were actors. Our casting director traveled around the country to Utah, Santa Fe, and other places to interview 400 young Navajo people. But we couldn't find anyone."

**Fun Facts**

- Beach enjoys playing ice hockey.
- His favorite kind of food is Chinese.
- He is learning to speak the language of the Saulteaux people and teaching it to his two sons.

Adam Beach plays a Native American boy named Victor Joseph in *Smoke Signals* (1998).

14    Woo was not willing to hire a weak actor just because he was Navajo. As Woo points out, "This is a very important role. It's not a supporting role. It's a main role." Luckily, he heard about Beach. Woo consulted with leaders of the Navajo tribe. He also checked with some of the real code talkers from World War II. After discussing it, they all agreed that Beach was the best one for the part, even though he was not Navajo.

15    In 2005 Beach began working on another World War II movie. This one was called *Flags of Our Fathers.* Directed by Clint Eastwood, it is based on the true story of the six men who raised the flag at Iwo Jima. One of those men was Ira Hayes, a Pima Indian, played in the movie by Beach.

16    Beach always looks for these types of roles. "I find myself searching for the right characters and the right stories," he says. "I have been, over the years, trying to do roles that show us as people in society and not just a Hollywood Indian." This attitude has served Adam Beach well, and he is now one of the most respected Native American actors in the business.

# A  Understanding What You Read

◆ **Fill in the circle next to the correct answer or write the answer.**

**1.** When Beach was seven years old he

○ A. took a drama class.

○ B. became an orphan.

○ C. played in a band.

**2.** In which paragraph did you find the information to answer question 1?

_____

**3.** Choose from the letters below to correctly complete the following statement. Write the letters on the lines.

In the article, _____ and _____ are alike.

A. Adam Beach

B. Clint Eastwood

C. Johnny Depp

**4.** According to the article, Beach has made more than one movie about

○ A. Squanto.

○ B. World War II.

○ C. Hollywood.

**5.** The author probably wrote this article in order to

○ A. make the reader laugh about what Adam Beach did.

○ B. talk the reader into studying Native American history.

○ C. tell the reader about a famous Native American actor.

_____ Number of Correct Answers: Part A

## Understanding Cause and Effect

◆ **Read the paragraph below. The paragraph shows cause and effect. The cause is that Beach saw Johnny Depp acting on** *21 Jump Street*. **Fill in the circle next to the sentence that shows the effect.**

**1.**

Beach got an added boost by watching Johnny Depp on the TV show *21 Jump Street*. Depp is part Cherokee. Beach thought that if Depp could be a professional actor, then maybe he could be one too.

○ A. Johnny Depp is part Cherokee.
○ B. Beach thought he could be an actor too.
○ C. Beach tried out for a role on *21 Jump Street*.

◆ **Reread paragraph 14 in the article. The paragraph shows cause and effect. The effect is that Woo was not willing to hire a weak actor just because he was Navajo. What question can you ask to find the cause? Write the question and the cause on the lines below.**

**2.** Question: _____

_____

Cause: _____

_____

_____ Number of Correct Answers: Part B

## C Using Words

◆ The words and phrases in the list below relate to the words in the box. Some words or phrases in the list have a meaning that is the same as or similar to a word in the box. Some have the opposite meaning. Write the related word from the box on each line. Use each word from the box twice.

| | | |
|---|---|---|
| aboriginal | bitter | complex |
| stereotyped | disapproved | |

### Same or similar meaning

**1.** complicated _____

**2.** native _____

**3.** did not accept _____

**4.** sorted by type _____

**5.** angry _____

**6.** grouped _____

### Opposite meaning

**7.** simple _____

**8.** agreed _____

**9.** happy _____

**10.** new arrival _____

_____ Number of Correct Answers: Part C

**D  Writing About It**

**Write a Movie Review**

◆ Write a review of Adam Beach's acting in the movie
*Windtalkers*. Finish the sentences below to write your review.
Use the checklist on page 103 to check your work.

The movie *Windtalkers* is a true story about _____

_____.

In the movie, Adam Beach plays _____

_____.

In real life, Beach is not Navajo. He is Saulteaux. He was hired for

the movie because _____

_____.

I think Beach was the right choice for the role because _____

_____

_____.

---

**Lesson 5** Add your correct answers from parts A, B, and C to get your total
score. Then find the percentage for your total score on the chart below.
Record your percentage on the graph on page 105.

_____ Total Score for Parts A, B, and C

_____ Percentage

| Total Score | 1 | 2 | 3 | 4 | 5 | 6 | 7 | 8 | 9 | 10 | 11 | 12 | 13 | 14 | 15 | 16 | 17 |
|---|---|---|---|---|---|---|---|---|---|---|---|---|---|---|---|---|---|
| Percentage | 6 | 12 | 18 | 24 | 29 | 35 | 41 | 47 | 53 | 59 | 65 | 71 | 76 | 82 | 88 | 94 | 100 |

# Jet Li
## Lights, Camera, Action!

**Birth Name** Jet Li Lian Jie

**Birth Date and Place** April 26, 1963; Beijing, China

**Homes** Beijing, China; Los Angeles, California; and other cities

# Think About What You Know

Do you think movies can teach people valuable lessons? What lessons can martial arts movies teach? Read the article to find out why Jet Li wants to make movies that have a message.

# Word Power

What do the words below tell you about the article?

**agility** the ability to move quickly and easily

**coordinated** skillful at moving different parts of the body at the same time

**saber** a heavy sword with a curved blade

**villain** the most important bad character in a movie or story

**violence** forceful actions that cause harm to people or objects

# Reading Skill

**Making Predictions** A **prediction** is a good guess about what will happen later in a story or article. Good readers make predictions based on clues from the text and what they already know. Good readers change their predictions as they read more of the story or article.

**Example**

On the first day of my martial arts class, we practiced stretching and breathing. A student asked the teacher when we would start learning to kick and fight. The teacher smiled and said, "Fighting is only a small part of martial arts. To stop your opponent without fighting is the greatest skill."

From the information in the paragraph, you can predict that *the students are going to learn more than just how to fight.* One clue to make this prediction is "we practiced stretching and breathing." What other clue helps you make this prediction? How does what you already know help you use the clues?

# Jet Li

## Lights, Camera, Action!

Jet Li is not your usual action hero. As a martial arts expert, he knows how to hit, kick, spin, jump, and block. In movies such as *Lethal Weapon 4* and *Kiss of the Dragon,* he demonstrates amazing strength and **agility.** His fight scenes are some of the best martial arts scenes ever filmed.

2     Li is more than just an actor who knows how to throw a punch. He is a thoughtful man who likes to ponder the big questions in life. What makes someone a hero? he wonders. Can violence be used to stop violence?

3     Jet Li's early years were spent in Beijing, China. The youngest of five children, he was only two years old when his father died. After that, his mother became very protective. She refused to let Li learn to ride a bicycle because she feared he would get hurt.

4     Not surprisingly, Li developed into a shy and timid boy. Despite his shyness, there was no mistaking Li's physical talent. His classroom teacher noticed how graceful and **coordinated** he was. The teacher recommended that Li attend a summer program to learn martial arts. So, at the age of eight, he began to study *Wushu,* which is called *kung fu* in the United States.

5     Li was so good at *Wushu* that when summer ended, he was transferred from his regular school to a special sports school. He still had to study reading, math, and science, but now he also spent eight hours each day learning *Wushu.* His instructor was a man named Wu Bin. Seeing that Li had special talent, Wu Bin became determined to mold him into a champion.

6    Wu Bin set higher standards for Li than for everyone else. When the other students were tired, they were allowed to rest, but when Li was tired, he had to keep going. Wu Bin forced Li to perform three times as many exercises as anyone else. No matter how hard Li worked, Wu Bin pushed him to work harder.

7    At times this made Li miserable, but it also made him strong. Over the next three years, Li developed dazzling moves. At the age of 12, he won China's national *Wushu* championship. He went on to win it for the next four years. At one of these competitions, Li accidentally cut his head with his **saber.** Blood poured from the wound, but Li was too focused to notice. He assumed the blood was just sweat. Incidents such as this one made him famous. By the time he was a teenager, Li was known and respected throughout his country.

8    When Li was 17, filmmakers convinced him to make a movie. *Shaolin Temple* was a huge success in China and led to a surge of interest in kung fu movies. Over the next 20 years, Li made many movies in China and Hong Kong. *Once Upon a Time in China* (1991) is considered one of the best martial arts films ever made. *Fist of Legend* (1994) is another classic.

9    In 1998 at the age of 35, Li released his first American movie: *Lethal Weapon 4* starring Mel Gibson. By then Li had made 25 films. In each one he had played a hero. In *Lethal Weapon 4,* he played a **villain** for the first time. Li did such a magnificent job that his picture was added to the movie poster soon after the film opened.

**Fun Facts**

- Li enjoys reading and playing table tennis.
- His favorite color is white.
- For four years after Li moved to the United States, he studied English four hours every day.

10   Next Li starred in *Romeo Must Die* (2000), *The One* (2001), and *Kiss of the Dragon* (2001). These movies helped propel him to the top of his field in the United States, earning him up to $10 million per film. To many people, it looked as though Li had it made, but that's not how he saw things.

11   Knowing that many young people looked up to him, Li worried about the **violence** in his films. He even issued a public warning urging parents not to bring their children to see *Kiss of the Dragon*. It wasn't just the violence. Li was no longer enjoying making martial arts movies. "I'd been learning martial arts for 30 years," he says, "and I was tired."

12   As a practicing Buddhist, Li spent a lot of time asking himself deep questions and seeking answers. He went to his Buddhist teacher and told him that he was thinking of retiring. The teacher did not respond as Li expected. Instead the teacher said, "You have a responsibility. You should continue." Li asked what his responsibility was. "You must figure that out yourself," said his teacher.

13   After much thought, Li decided his responsibility was to help teach his fans important lessons. As he puts it, some of these fans "are little boys. Some are teenagers. Maybe they haven't found their way in life yet. I feel if I can share some information, it can help them."

## Skill Break
### Making Predictions

Look at paragraphs 12 and 13 on this page. Using clues in these paragraphs, what do you think is most likely to **happen next?**

What **clues** did you use to make your prediction?

How did **what you already know** help you use the clues?

As you read the next page, check to see if what happens next matches your prediction.

Jet Li (right) and Russell Wong share a fight scene in the movie *Romeo Must Die*.

14  After that, Li looked for more meaningful roles. "I think if people want to watch Jet Li's films, I still need to have fights," he says. But "through the fight I can tell different kinds of stories."

15  This new way of looking at his work led Li to make *Hero* in 2002. In his mind, it is not just an action film. It is "wider than that," he says. "It talks about peace and what kind of Chinese people can become heroes." Li hoped the movie would help teach his audience about Chinese culture and beliefs.

16  *Unleashed,* another movie that has special meaning for him, came out in 2005. Li says, "I wanted to make this film to talk to people." His message is that you can know martial arts very well, but that's not enough if you don't "understand life." "That's the whole meaning of the movie," he says. "Violence is not the only solution."

17  Li points out that "in real life, I never fight with people." He values peace. He says, "My hope is for us to become one world of peace without having to give up the things that we believe in. I want my fighting to be in the movies, not in life."

# A  Understanding What You Read

◆ **Fill in the circle next to the correct answer.**

**1.** Li accidentally cut his head during

- ○ A. a practice fight with Wu Bin.
- ○ B. the filming of *Fist of Legend*.
- ○ C. a Chinese *Wushu* competition.

**2.** From what you read in the article, you can conclude that *Wushu*

- ○ A. is only practiced by actors.
- ○ B. can sometimes be dangerous.
- ○ C. started in the United States.

**3.** In the movie *Lethal Weapon 4,* Li plays a

- ○ A. villain.
- ○ B. detective.
- ○ C. hero.

**4.** How is Jet Li an example of a good role model?

- ○ A. He was only two years old when his father died.
- ○ B. He has made many violent martial arts movies.
- ○ C. He uses his movies to teach important lessons.

**5.** What sentence **best** states the main idea of the article?

- ○ A. Li is a skilled martial arts master and film star.
- ○ B. Li's movies are well-known around the world.
- ○ C. Li started learning *Wushu* at a young age.

_____ Number of Correct Answers: Part A

**Making Predictions**

◆ Read the paragraph below. Look at the clues in the paragraph. Fill in the circle next to the prediction that is **most likely** to happen based on the clues.

**1.**

Wu Bin set higher standards for Li than for everyone else. When the other students were tired, they were allowed to rest, but when Li was tired, he had to keep going. Wu Bin forced Li to perform three times as many exercises as anyone else. No matter how hard Li worked, Wu Bin pushed him to work harder.

○ A. Wu Bin will send Li on a vacation.
○ B. Wu Bin will decide to stop teaching Li.
○ C. Wu Bin's teaching will help Li improve.

◆ What clues in the paragraph helped you make the prediction? How did what you already know help you make the prediction? Write **at least two** clues and what you already know on the lines.

**2.** Clues: _____

_____

_____

What I Know: _____

_____

_____ Number of Correct Answers: Part B

# C Using Words

◆ Complete each sentence with a word from the box. Write the missing word on the line.

| | | |
|---|---|---|
| agility | saber | violence |
| coordinated | villain | |

**1.** The war movie had a lot of _____ in it.

**2.** By the end of the story, the _____ saw that what he had done was wrong.

**3.** As she became more _____, she became a better skier.

**4.** The ballet dancer had great _____.

**5.** In ancient China, a warrior might use a _____ to defend himself.

◆ Choose one word from the box. Write a new sentence using the word.

**6.** word: _____

_____

_____

_____ Number of Correct Answers: Part C

## D  Writing About It

### Write a Comic Strip

◆ Write a comic strip about Jet Li. First look at what is happening in each scene. Think about what each person might be saying. Then finish the sentence in each bubble. Use the checklist on page 103 to check your work.

THIS YOUNG BOY HAS _____ _____. I WOULD LIKE TO _____

YAH!

I AM SO TIRED! WU BIN ALWAYS

**Lesson 6** Add your correct answers from parts A, B, and C to get your total score. Then find the percentage for your total score on the chart below. Record your percentage on the graph on page 105.

_____ Total Score for Parts A, B, and C

_____ Percentage

| Total Score | 1 | 2 | 3 | 4 | 5 | 6 | 7 | 8 | 9 | 10 | 11 | 12 | 13 |
|---|---|---|---|---|---|---|---|---|---|---|---|---|---|
| Percentage | 8 | 15 | 23 | 31 | 38 | 46 | 54 | 62 | 69 | 77 | 85 | 92 | 100 |

# Compare and Contrast

◆ Think about the celebrities, or famous people, in Unit Two. Pick two articles that tell about celebrities who showed talent at a young age and who use their talent in a positive way. Use information from the articles to fill in this chart.

| Celebrity's Name | | |
|---|---|---|
| What talent did the celebrity show at a young age? | | |
| When and how did the celebrity first show the talent? | | |
| How does the celebrity use the talent in a positive way? | | |

Beyoncé

Denzel Washington

Carly Patterson

# Beyoncé

## Driven to Become a Star

**Birth Name** Beyoncé Giselle Knowles

**Birth Date and Place** September 4, 1981; Houston, Texas

**Home** Miami, Florida

# Think About What You Know

Do you feel like most people you know understand who you really are?
Have you ever done something that was misunderstood by others?
Read the article and find out why Beyoncé feels like people do not
understand who she really is.

# Word Power

What do the words below tell you about the article?

**categorize** to classify or put into a specific group

**distorted** changed in a way that makes something unclear or inaccurate

**strenuous** needing great effort

**citing** using as a reason or example

**critics** people who talk about someone's faults

# Reading Skill

**Using Context** **Context clues** can help you find the meaning of a word
that you don't understand. Context clues are other words in the same
sentence or in nearby sentences. If you don't understand a word, look for
clues around it that might help you. Then try to find the meaning.

**Example**

**Context Clues**

**New Word**

    I enjoy talking to people. That's because I am very
outgoing. I love to meet new people, and I like getting
a lot of attention. Someday I might become a famous
performer.

If you don't know the meaning of the word *outgoing,* you can use
the context clues "talking to people," "love to meet new people,"
and "like getting a lot of attention" to help you find the meaning.
From these clues, what do you think *outgoing* means?

# Beyoncé
## Driven to Become a Star

Beyoncé Knowles is a complicated young woman. On the one hand, she's a sizzling pop star who wears wild outfits and makes flashy music videos. On the other hand, she's a deeply religious person who prays daily and will fly thousands of miles to attend her hometown church service. Although her behavior makes it difficult for people to **categorize** her, Beyoncé has no plans to change who she is or what she does. After all, she knows that the public often gets **distorted** ideas about famous people. She just wants her fans to enjoy her performances. She hopes that fans will come to realize that her public image is very different from her private self.

2    Beyoncé's career began when she was very young. At age seven, she already loved to sing and dance. Her parents, Tina and Matthew Knowles, began entering her in local talent contests. Beyoncé won 35 contests in a row. When she was nine, her parents teamed her with two other girls to form the group Girls Tyme. Later a fourth girl joined the group and it became Destiny's Child.

3    Many people have accused her parents of being overly involved in their daughter's career. They certainly have focused a lot of time and energy on Beyoncé. Tina reduced the hours she spent on her hairdressing business in order to become the group's hairstylist and costume designer. Matthew was committed to the quest of making his child a star. To reach that goal, he quit his job and became Beyoncé's manager. He hired a voice coach to live with the family, and he built a practice stage in the family's backyard.

4    Beyoncé admits that the schedule her father set up and the tough training sessions he arranged were sometimes grueling. "My dad would have us jogging and singing in harmony," she recalls. "It was pretty harsh. We were able to do cartwheels and sing . . . It's definitely difficult, but you do it."

5    Whether people approve of the way Matthew and Tina coached their daughter or not, their methods did get results. Destiny's Child became an enormously successful group. Beyoncé in particular grew into a young woman with a voice so unusually beautiful that many people found it stunning. Thanks to her father's training, she was able to belt out songs even while performing **strenuous** dance routines. Many stars will record a song ahead of time and then lip-synch to the recording while they dance, but Beyoncé doesn't need the help. As she says, "I've been dancing and singing since I was nine."

6    In 1997 Columbia Records signed a recording contract with Destiny's Child. That same year, the group released its first single, "No, No, No." The song went straight to the top of the charts, paving the way for their self-titled first album, which sold a million copies. The group's second album, *The Writing's on the Wall,* sold nine million copies.

## Skill Break
### Using Context
Look at paragraph 5 on this page. Find the word *stunning* in the middle of the paragraph.

What **clue** in the paragraph can help you find the meaning of *stunning*?

From the clue, what do you think *stunning* means?

7    Destiny's Child was becoming one of the biggest selling female acts of all time. There was trouble in the group, though. In 2000, two members of the group left and filed a lawsuit. They claimed that the group's management—and in particular Matthew Knowles—had been unfair to them and had made Beyoncé's career a higher priority than their own. Eventually the issue was resolved out of court. A deal was agreed upon, and the two unhappy young women left the group. Two new performers joined, but one only lasted a few months. She soon left the group, **citing** the same problems that the earlier two had described.

8    These conflicts could have destroyed Destiny's Child, but they didn't. Beyoncé and the two remaining members of the group, Kelly Rowland and newcomer Michelle Williams, turned Destiny's Child into a trio. They released *Survivor* in 2001 and *Destiny Fulfilled* in 2004. Both albums were big successes.

9    The lawsuit was not the end of the bad publicity, however. The press continued to talk about Beyoncé. People found other things to criticize about her. Some did not like the costumes she wore. Others didn't like her talking so openly about her religion. Some thought she gave her father too much power. Others complained about her choice of boyfriends. Still others thought her public efforts to stay thin made her a bad role model for teenage girls.

**Fun Facts**

▶ One of the first songs Beyoncé ever performed on stage was the John Lennon song "Imagine."

▶ She enjoys oil painting.

▶ In 2001 she won the Songwriter of the Year Award from a well-known music society. She was the first African American woman to win the award.

Beyoncé Knowles performs at Radio City Music Hall in New York City.

10    Beyoncé responded by explaining the difference between her public image and her private self. "Beyoncé the performer" was the one who wore revealing outfits. The private Beyoncé was happier in baggy pants and a T-shirt. The public Beyoncé might appear cool and confident, but the private Beyoncé was warm, friendly, and humble. "Maybe I should use a different name for Beyoncé the performer," she said. "The two of us are so different."

11    Beyoncé knows that criticism goes along with being famous, and she accepts that. She wishes that **critics** would acknowledge her talents, though. The range of her singing voice is amazing—and she doesn't just sing songs, she writes them too. With her 2003 solo album *Dangerously in Love,* she proved she can stand alone as a performer. She also received praise and complimentary reviews for her acting in the 2002 Austin Powers' movie *Goldmember.*

12    No matter what the critics say, Beyoncé is comfortable with who she is and what she has done. "You . . . have to get up in the morning and be happy within yourself," she says. She adds, "I'm the same girl that I was before all this started, just a little older and a lot wiser."

# A ⬛ Understanding What You Read

◆ **Fill in the circle next to the correct answer.**

**1.** What was the cause of young Beyoncé entering talent contests when she was a child?

○ A. She was planning to become famous.
○ B. She was in the group Girls Tyme.
○ C. She loved to sing and dance.

**2.** Which of the following statements is an opinion rather than a fact?

○ A. Tina reduced her hours at her business.
○ B. Matthew quit his job to manage Beyoncé.
○ C. Tina and Matthew were too involved.

**3.** Two members of Destiny's Child left the group because

○ A. they felt they were not treated fairly.
○ B. their albums were not selling well.
○ C. the group decided to become a trio.

**4.** When Beyoncé is not performing, she likes to wear

○ A. a lot of makeup.
○ B. baggy pants.
○ C. wild costumes.

**5.** From the information in the article, you can predict that Beyoncé will

○ A. start using taped vocals when she performs.
○ B. make another successful solo album.
○ C. hire a new manager to work with her.

_____ Number of Correct Answers: Part A

# B Using Context

◆ Read the paragraph below. Look for context clues that tell you what the word *grueling* means. Underline **at least two** context clues in the paragraph. Then fill in the circle next to the correct meaning of *grueling*.

**1.**

Beyoncé admits that the schedule her father set up and the tough training sessions he arranged were sometimes grueling. "My dad would have us jogging and singing in harmony," she recalls. "It was pretty harsh. We were able to do cartwheels and sing . . . It's definitely difficult, but you do it."

○ A. very short
○ B. very unusual
○ C. very difficult

◆ Reread paragraph 9 in the article. Find the word *criticize* in the middle of the paragraph. Look for context clues about the meaning of *criticize*. Write **two** clues on the lines below. Then write what you think *criticize* means.

**2.** Context Clues: _____

_____

*Criticize* means: _____

_____

_____ Number of Correct Answers: Part B

# C  Using Words

◆ Cross out one of the four words in each row that does **not** relate to the word in dark type.

**1. categorize**

sort            hide            label           list

**2. distorted**

mistaken        false           simple          different

**3. strenuous**

struggle        tired           energy          folded

**4. citing**

admire          explain         mention         prove

**5. critics**

judge           create          comment         approve

◆ Choose one of the words shown in dark type above. Write a sentence using the word.

**6.** word: _____

_____

_____

_____ Number of Correct Answers: Part C

## D  Writing About It

### Write an Advertisement

◆ Write an advertisement for a Beyoncé concert. Finish the
sentences below to write your advertisement. Use the checklist
on page 103 to check your work.

*Tickets on Sale*

# See Beyoncé Live in Concert!

Come see Beyoncé perform at a solo show. Many people know Beyoncé

from _____

_____ .

Beyoncé amazes her audiences with _____

_____ .

Unlike some other live performers who sing and dance, _____

_____ .

Don't miss this great show!

*Tickets on Sale*

**Lesson 7** Add your correct answers from parts A, B, and C to get your total
score. Then find the percentage for your total score on the chart below.
Record your percentage on the graph on page 105.

_____ Total Score for Parts A, B, and C

_____ Percentage

| Total Score | 1 | 2 | 3 | 4 | 5 | 6 | 7 | 8 | 9 | 10 | 11 | 12 | 13 |
|---|---|---|---|---|---|---|---|---|---|---|---|---|---|
| Percentage | 8 | 15 | 23 | 31 | 38 | 46 | 54 | 62 | 69 | 77 | 85 | 92 | 100 |

# Denzel Washington
## Keeping It Simple

**Birth Name** Denzel Washington

**Birth Date and Place** December 28, 1954; Mount Vernon, New York

**Home** Beverly Hills, California

# Think About What You Know

Would you like to live a fancy life with many luxuries, or would you prefer to live a simple life? Read the article and find out what kind of life Denzel Washington chooses for himself.

# Word Power

What do the words below tell you about the article?

**activist** someone who takes action to try to change something

**quadriplegic** someone who is permanently unable to move his or her arms, legs, and torso

**negative** bad or harmful

**journalism** the work of researching and writing news reports

**arrogant** feeling or acting overly proud or superior

# Reading Skill

**Cause and Effect** Many stories and articles show cause and effect. A **cause** tells *why* something happened. An **effect** tells *what* happened. The cause happens first. Then, as a result, the effect happens. The clue word *because* can help you find the cause. The clue words *so* and *as a result* can help you find the effect. Asking *What happened as a result?* can also help you find the effect.

| Example | |
|---|---|
| **Cause** | The actor didn't think she would get much work |
| **Effect** | in her small town, so she moved to Hollywood. |

"The actor didn't think she would get much work in her small town" is the cause. "She moved to Hollywood" is the effect. The clue word *so* comes before the effect. Another way to find the effect is to ask *What happened as a result? What happened as a result* of the actor thinking she couldn't get much work in her small town?

# Denzel Washington

## Keeping It Simple

Denzel Washington has done it all. During his 30-year acting career, he has played everything from a criminal to an angel. He's been a police officer, a psychologist, and a military man. He has portrayed a South African **activist** and an African American activist. He has appeared as a lawyer, a boxer, a football coach, and even a **quadriplegic** police detective.

2   Along the way, Washington has won dozens of awards, including Academy Awards for Best Actor and Best Supporting Actor. He is so widely sought after that he has to turn down countless movie offers every year. He has become one of the most famous actors in the world.

3   Washington grew up in New York. He says that living in his childhood neighborhood was "a good background for somebody in my business." He says, "My friends were West Indian, Blacks, Irish, and Italians, so I learned a lot about different cultures."

4   Because Washington's father was a minister and his mother managed a beauty shop, he spent plenty of time watching, listening to, and talking to all sorts of people. These experiences served him well when he became an actor. However, he admits, "I could very easily have been caught up in the streets. I almost was."

5   When Washington was 14 years old, his parents split up and his father left. As a result, Washington started to spend more time on the streets. His grades dropped and he began getting into fights. "There was fear," he recalls, "and there was danger. There were four of us who hung out together. And of the other three . . . one died of AIDS from shooting up drugs, one was murdered, and the other is doing 25-years-to-life in jail."

6    Washington's mother felt that this dangerous environment would have a **negative** effect on her son's future. So she got enough money together to send Washington to a private school. There he focused his energy on better things, becoming active in sports and getting high enough grades to get into Fordham University.

7    When he started college, Washington wanted to become a doctor. When he didn't do well in the classes, he switched to **journalism.** That didn't last long, either. Washington was bored at the city council meetings he had to attend. "Item number 16 . . . parking meters . . . blah blah blah," he says. "I fell asleep."

8    It wasn't until Washington took a summer job as a camp counselor that his future became clearer. He organized a talent contest for the campers and did a short performance in it himself. Not only did he enjoy it but also everyone told him he was wonderful. In the fall, he tried out for a play and signed up for a theater workshop. By the time he graduated from college, he knew he wanted to act.

9    Washington spent the next year studying at the American Conservatory Theater in San Francisco. Then he moved to Los Angeles to look for work. He won a role in a TV movie called *Wilma,* based on the life of Olympic track star Wilma Rudolph. It was while making this movie that he met Pauletta Pearson, who became his wife and the mother of their four children.

## Skill Break
### Cause and Effect

Look at paragraph 6 on this page. This paragraph shows cause and effect.

The **cause** is that Washington's mother felt that the dangerous environment would not be good for her son's future. What is the **effect?**

What **clue word** can help you find the effect?

What **question** could you ask to help you find the effect?

10   Washington's first Hollywood movie came in 1981, when he appeared in *Carbon Copy.* The movie didn't get great reviews, but it helped launch Washington's big-screen career. The following year he took a role on *St. Elsewhere,* a TV series that ran for six years. During the show's season breaks, Washington made the impressive movies *A Soldier's Story* (1984) and *Cry Freedom* (1987).

11   Then Washington played a Civil War soldier in the 1989 movie *Glory.* The role won him the Academy Award for Best Supporting Actor. This award made Washington a big enough star to be able to accept only the movie roles that he really wanted. His reputation grew. Then in 2001, he won the Academy Award for Best Actor for his performance in *Training Day.*

12   Washington likes a challenge, and after acting in so many movies, he was eager to try something new. So in 2002, he tried directing for the first time and directed the movie *Antwone Fisher.* Three years later, he took a break from Hollywood altogether and did some theater. He acted in a Broadway production of Shakespeare's *Julius Caesar.*

13   With all of the success Washington has had, it wouldn't be surprising to find him a bit **arrogant.** He's not, though. He may be an intense actor, but he's a warm and down-to-earth person who doesn't need a lot of luxuries. "It just isn't me," he says. That's why he wears a $39 watch when he could afford a much more expensive one. "Why do I need to spend $50,000 on a watch when this one is just fine?" he asks. "I like to keep it simple."

**Fun Facts**

- Washington is a fan of the Los Angeles Lakers basketball team.
- He enjoys boxing.
- He named one of his sons Malcolm in honor of Malcolm X.
- He and his wife are part owners of a restaurant named Georgia.

14　　Washington almost never goes to Hollywood parties, either. He prefers to do "regular guy things like go over to a friend's house to barbecue or coach my son's basketball team." As he says, "I didn't get here from partying with the right people or doing anything other than working hard." So he keeps his focus on the things that matter to him, especially his family.

15　　The night Washington won the Academy Award for Best Actor, he couldn't wait to get home to share the victory with his family. When he stepped up to accept his award, he said, "My beautiful wife, I love you so much. My beautiful children at home, I told you, if I lost tonight, I'd come home and we'd celebrate it. If I won tonight, we'd come home and we'd celebrate. Well, we're coming home and we're celebrating."

16　　So while Washington is very proud of what he has accomplished as an actor, he makes it clear that his career is not the most important thing in his life. He says, "Family is life; acting is making a living."

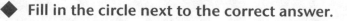
◆ **Fill in the circle next to the correct answer.**

**1.** When Washington said that his childhood neighborhood was "a good background for somebody in my business," he probably meant that

- ○ A. actors need to know about different kinds of people.
- ○ B. he met several movie stars while he was growing up.
- ○ C. a lot of movies take place in New York neighborhoods.

**2.** As a college student, Washington was bored when he attended

- ○ A. camp talent contests.
- ○ B. city council meetings.
- ○ C. basketball games.

**3.** Washington said that if he lost the Academy Award for Best Actor he would

- ○ A. go to a friend's house to barbecue.
- ○ B. give up acting and become a director.
- ○ C. come home and celebrate with his family.

**4.** The author probably wrote this article in order to

- ○ A. explain to the reader how to get a role in a movie.
- ○ B. persuade the reader to watch the Academy Awards.
- ○ C. inform the reader about the career of a famous actor.

**5.** Which **best** states the lesson about life that this article teaches?

- ○ A. Your career should not keep you away from your family.
- ○ B. Being an actor is more rewarding than being a doctor.
- ○ C. Too much success can make a person arrogant.

_____ Number of Correct Answers: Part A

## B Understanding Cause and Effect

◆ **Read the paragraph below. The paragraph shows cause and effect. The cause is that Washington's father was a minister and his mother managed a beauty shop. Fill in the circle next to the sentence that shows the effect.**

**1.**

Because Washington's father was a minister and his mother managed a beauty shop, he spent plenty of time watching, listening to, and talking to all sorts of people. These experiences served him well when he became an actor. However, he admits, "I could very easily have been caught up in the streets. I almost was."

○ A. He listened to his parents and decided to become an actor.
○ B. He spent time watching, listening to, and talking to people.
○ C. He could very easily have been caught up in the streets.

◆ **Reread paragraph 12 in the article. The paragraph shows causes and effects. The causes are that Washington likes a challenge and he was eager to try something new. What question can you ask to help you find the effects? Write the question and two effects on the lines below.**

**2.** Question: _____

_____

Effects: _____

_____

_____ Number of Correct Answers: Part B

# C  Using Words

◆ Complete each sentence with a word from the box. Write the missing word on the line.

| | | |
|---|---|---|
| activist | negative | arrogant |
| quadriplegic | journalism | |

**1.** One _____ thing about eating sweets is that sweets can cause tooth decay.

**2.** The _____ girl ignored everyone who didn't seem as smart as she was.

**3.** The _____ author learned to write using his mouth.

**4.** A reporter visited our school to talk about her career in

_____ .

**5.** The _____ organized a rally to protest the new law.

◆ Choose one word from the box. Write a new sentence using the word.

**6.** word: _____

_____

_____

## D  Writing About It

### Write a Letter

◆ Write a letter to Denzel Washington. Finish the sentences below to write your letter. Use the checklist on page 103 to check your work.

Dear Mr. Washington,

I just read an article about you. I learned that you _____

_____.

I admire you because _____

_____.

I would like to know more about _____

_____.

Sincerely,

_____

**Lesson 8** Add your correct answers from parts A, B, and C to get your total score. Then find the percentage for your total score on the chart below. Record your percentage on the graph on page 105.

_____ Total Score for Parts A, B, and C

_____ Percentage

| Total Score | 1 | 2 | 3 | 4 | 5 | 6 | 7 | 8 | 9 | 10 | 11 | 12 | 13 |
|---|---|---|---|---|---|---|---|---|---|---|---|---|---|
| Percentage | 8 | 15 | 23 | 31 | 38 | 46 | 54 | 62 | 69 | 77 | 85 | 92 | 100 |

# Carly Patterson
## One Tough Gymnast

**Birth Name** Carly Rae Patterson

**Birth Date and Place** February 4, 1988; Baton Rouge, Louisiana

**Home** Allen, Texas

# Think About What You Know

Have you ever performed in front of a large group? How did you feel? Read the article to find out about Carly Patterson and her championship gymnastics performances.

# Word Power

What do the words below tell you about the article?

**uninspired** not showing any creativity or excitement

**deducted** took away a part of something

**penalty** a punishment for breaking a rule

**rival** a person that someone competes with

**ligament** a strong material in the body that holds bones or organs in place

# Reading Skill

**Making Predictions** A **prediction** is a good guess about what will happen later in a story or article. Good readers make predictions based on clues from the text and what they already know. Good readers change their predictions as they read more of the story or article.

### Example

On Mondays and Wednesdays, I have gymnastics class. On Tuesdays and Thursdays, I have drama club. On Fridays I volunteer at a hospital. On Saturdays and Sundays, I play soccer. Lately I've been thinking about signing up for an art class.

From the information in the paragraph, you can predict that *the author will probably not have time to take an art class*. One clue to make this prediction is "On Mondays and Wednesdays, I have gymnastics class." What other clues tell you that the writer will probably not have time to take an art class? How does what you already know help you use these clues?

# Carly Patterson

## One Tough Gymnast

This was the moment of truth. If Carly Patterson made any more mistakes, it would mean the end of her dream. It was August 19, 2004, and Patterson was in the middle of the Olympic Games in Athens, Greece. The 16-year-old Patterson had come to Athens hoping to win the Women's Individual All-Around Artistic Gymnastics competition. The U.S. team was counting on her to get the highest total score for vault, uneven bars, balance beam, and floor exercise.

2   Patterson had started out poorly, though. Her vaulting had been shaky, and her performance on the uneven bars had been **uninspired.** Now instead of being in first place, Patterson found herself in fourth. Only two events remained: the balance beam and the floor exercise. Unless she did well on both events, there would be no All-Around gold medal hanging from Patterson's neck.

3   Performing at the highest level of gymnastics is always stressful. Even minor mistakes can ruin the chance for a medal—and so many things can go wrong. An error on the balance beam, a misstep on the floor exercise, or a slip on the uneven bars—any of these things—can mean the difference between a top finish and a bad day. On Patterson's vault, for instance, she had accidentally stepped outside the lines in the landing area. As a result, two-tenths of a point had been **deducted** from her score. Two-tenths of a point might not seem like much, but in the world of Olympic gymnastics it's a harsh **penalty.**

4   The Olympics attract the best gymnasts in the world. Out of a perfect score of 10.0, top competitors are expected to score above 9.5. So Patterson's score of 9.375 for vault was disappointing.

5    Luckily for Patterson, her biggest **rival** didn't do much better. Russia's Svetlana Khorkina wobbled on the landing of her vault, scoring 9.462. Khorkina was wonderful on the bars, though, outscoring Patterson by .15. Patterson could still move ahead, but only if she performed brilliantly in the last two events.

6    The balance beam was next. It was Patterson's favorite event, but in the U.S. Olympic trials, she had fallen off twice. She couldn't have a disaster like that tonight. Her routine had to be close to perfect. Somehow she had to find the strength and the focus to avoid errors and show the judges how good she could be.

7    It takes great mental toughness to perform well with so much at risk, but, as anyone who knows Patterson will tell you, she is tough. "She's a very competitive girl," says her personal coach, Evgeny Marchenko. "After she makes a mistake, she fights back."

8    "She is able to perform the best when the moment comes that is the most important," agrees U.S. team coordinator Marta Karolyi.

9    Patterson had shown how tough she could be back at the 2003 World Championships. During a warm-up session, she injured her elbow. "It swelled up and was really throbbing," she recalls. Rubbing it and putting ice on it didn't relieve the pain. Patterson refused to see a doctor, though. "I didn't want to find out what was wrong because I knew they'd tell me not to compete," she says. "So I just tried to block it out and keep pushing myself."

**Fun Facts**

- Patterson began doing gymnastics when she was six years old.
- When she is training for a competition, Patterson practices 35 hours per week.
- She has a beautiful singing voice and has been recording some of her own pop and rock music.

10    Ignoring the pain, Patterson continued to perform. By the end of the competition, she couldn't even straighten her arm out all the way. But by the time the Championships were over, she had helped her team finish in first place and had won second place in the individual all-around competition. Only then did she go to the doctor. As she'd suspected, the injury was serious. Her elbow was fractured on both sides, and a **ligament** was damaged. She needed three hours of surgery to repair everything.

11    So as she stood in the Olympic stadium in 2004, Patterson knew she once again had to rise to the occasion. And that's exactly what she did. She performed an outstanding beam routine that ended with a dismount she invented herself. The dismount starts with a round-off, back handspring and ends with a double Arabian front flip. Because she is the first person ever to complete this move in competition, it is called the Patterson.

12    Patterson received a score of 9.725 for her beam routine. That put her back in the race for the gold. "She had her greatest minute at the right time, at the most important time," said famous Olympic coach Bela Karolyi. "She delivered a perfect routine." Khorkina, meanwhile, wobbled a couple of times during her beam routine and received a score of just 9.462. Suddenly Patterson was ahead, though only by .026. The floor exercise would decide it all.

## Skill Break
### Making Predictions

Look at paragraph 12 on this page. Using clues in the paragraph, what do you think is most likely to **happen next?**

What **clues** did you use to make your prediction?

How did **what you already know** help you use the clues?

As you read the next page, check to see if what happens next matches your prediction.

**Carly Patterson performs a jump during her balance-beam routine at the 2004 Summer Olympics. She won the silver medal in the event.**

13    Khorkina went first, performing a floor routine that was beautiful but had a bit too much dance. It included only three tumbling passes. The judges gave her a score of 9.562. When Patterson's turn came, she held nothing back. Showing no signs of nervousness, she bounded confidently across the floor, thrilling the crowd with four strong tumbling passes. As soon as her music ended, she knew she had done it. She had won the gold medal.

14    Coming off the mat, Patterson threw her arms around Coach Marchenko, tears streaming down her face. When her score of 9.712 was posted, it became official. Patterson had won the gold medal by .176.

15    "I'm so excited and happy," she told reporters. "I'm just overwhelmed right now. I just can't even believe it yet. I'm [going to] have to sleep on it."

16    "You couldn't create more pressure," said Marchenko. "She handled it very well, and that's what she's famous for. She proved it here." As he put it, "If you're not mentally tough, you're not the Olympic champion."

# A  Understanding What You Read

◆ **Fill in the circle next to the correct answer or write the answer.**

**1.** Patterson went to Athens in 2004 hoping to

   ○ A. talk with Svetlana Khorkina.

   ○ B. win an All-Around gold medal.

   ○ C. keep her elbow injury a secret.

**2.** Choose from the letters below to correctly complete the following statement. Write the letters on the lines.

   On the bad side, _____, but on the good side, _____.

   A. Patterson's floor routine at the Olympics was strong

   B. Patterson's vaulting at the Olympics was shaky

   C. Patterson had a fall on her final Olympic beam routine

**3.** When she is under pressure, Patterson

   ○ A. usually performs well.

   ○ B. often gets nervous.

   ○ C. always asks for help.

**4.** From what the article told you about gymnastics, you can conclude that

   ○ A. most gymnasts prefer the vault over the beam.

   ○ B. the uneven bars is the most exciting event.

   ○ C. a floor routine includes both dance and tumbling.

**5.** In which paragraph did you find the information to answer question 4?

   _____

_____ Number of Correct Answers: Part A

## B Making Predictions

◆ Read the paragraph below. Look at the clues in each paragraph. Fill in the circle next to the prediction that is **most likely** to happen based on the clues.

**1.**

Patterson had shown how tough she could be back at the 2003 World Championships. During a warm-up session, she injured her elbow. "It swelled up and was really throbbing," she recalls. Rubbing it and putting ice on it didn't relieve the pain. Patterson refused to see a doctor, though. "I didn't want to find out what was wrong because I knew they'd tell me not to compete," she says. "So I just tried to block it out and keep pushing myself."

○ A. Patterson's parents will find out and make her go to the doctor.
○ B. Patterson will use more ice and her elbow will stop hurting.
○ C. Patterson will ignore the pain and finish the competition.

◆ What clues in the paragraph helped you make the prediction? How did what you already know help you make the prediction? Write **at least two** clues and what you already know on the lines.

**2.** Clues: _____

_____

_____

What I Know: _____

_____

_____ Number of Correct Answers: Part B

# C  Using Words

◆ The words and phrases in the list below relate to the words in
the box. Some words or phrases in the list have a meaning that
is the same as or similar to a word in the box. Some have the
opposite meaning. Write the related word from the box on
each line. Use each word from the box twice.

| | | |
|---|---|---|
| uninspired | penalty | ligament |
| deducted | rival | |

## Same or similar meaning

**1.** opponent _____

**2.** bone wrapping _____

**3.** punishment _____

**4.** dull _____

**5.** subtracted _____

**6.** connecting material _____

## Opposite meaning

**7.** added _____

**8.** enthusiastic _____

**9.** reward _____

**10.** partner _____

_____ Number of Correct Answers: Part C

# D  Writing About It

## Write a Scene from a Play

◆ Write a scene from a play about Carly Patterson. The scene takes place at the 2004 Olympic Games. Finish the sentences below to write your scene. Use the checklist on page 103 to check your work.

*(Patterson has just completed her beam routine at the 2004 Olympics.)*

**Coach Marchenko:** Nice job, Carly! Your beam routine _____

_____.

**Patterson:** Look, they're showing my score. It's 9.725!

**Coach Marchenko:** That means _____.

**Patterson:** The floor exercise is next. I'll have to _____

_____.

**Coach Marchenko:** Just stay focused. You still have a chance to

_____.

---

**Lesson 9** Add your correct answers from parts A, B, and C to get your total score. Then find the percentage for your total score on the chart below. Record your percentage on the graph on page 105.

_____ Total Score for Parts A, B, and C

_____ Percentage

| Total Score | 1 | 2 | 3 | 4 | 5 | 6 | 7 | 8 | 9 | 10 | 11 | 12 | 13 | 14 | 15 | 16 | 17 |
|---|---|---|---|---|---|---|---|---|---|---|---|---|---|---|---|---|---|
| Percentage | 6 | 12 | 18 | 24 | 29 | 35 | 41 | 47 | 53 | 59 | 65 | 71 | 76 | 82 | 88 | 94 | 100 |

# Compare and Contrast

◆ Think about the celebrities, or famous people, in Unit Three. Pick two articles that tell about celebrities who received help or support during their life. Use information from the articles to fill in this chart.

| Celebrity's Name | | |
|---|---|---|
| Who helped or supported the celebrity? | | |
| How did the person or people support the celebrity? | | |
| Would you like to be supported in the same way? Why or why not? | | |

# Glossary

## A

**aboriginal**   one of the first, or original, groups of people to live in an area   p. 46

**activist**   someone who takes action to try to change something   p. 78

**agility**   the ability to move quickly and easily   p. 56

**anthem**   a song that praises something, such as a team or a country   p. 6

**arrogant**   feeling or acting overly proud or superior   p. 80

## B

**bitter**   full of disappointment and bad feelings   p. 47

## C

**carefree**   without worries   p. 27

**categorize**   to classify or put into a specific group   p. 68

**citing**   using as a reason or example   p. 70

**collision**   two things crashing into one another   p. 15

**complex**   difficult to understand   p. 48

**conscious**   awake and aware   p. 25

**coordinated** skillful at moving different parts of the body at the
   same time   p. 56

**critics** people who talk about someone's faults   p. 71

# D

**deadline** a time or date when something must be finished   p. 26

**deducted** took away a part of something   p. 88

**disapproved** did not like or did not support what someone
   was doing   p. 48

**distorted** changed in a way that makes something unclear
   or inaccurate   p. 68

# E

**ego** pride or confidence in oneself   p. 38

**electrified** surprised and thrilled   p. 4

# G

**generator** a machine that creates electricity   p. 14

# H

**hull** the outer frame of a ship   p. 14

# J

**journalism** the work of researching and writing news reports   p. 79

# L

**landlocked**   completely surrounded by land with no large bodies of water nearby   p. 15

**ligament**   a strong material in the body that holds bones or organs in place   p. 90

**lurked**   moved around while staying hidden from view   p. 24

# M

**meditate**   to relax and become more aware of yourself, often done while sitting with eyes closed   p. 6

**miniature**   very small   p. 36

# N

**negative**   bad or harmful   p. 79

# O

**observer**   a person who is watching something carefully   p. 36

# P

**penalty**   a punishment for breaking a rule   p. 88

**phenomenal**   extraordinary or fantastic   p. 37

# Q

**quadriplegic**   someone who is permanently unable to move his or her arms, legs, and torso   p. 78

# R

**rehearsing**   practicing for a performance, such as a concert   p. 5

**rival**   a person that someone competes with   p. 89

# S

**saber**   a heavy sword with a curved blade   p. 57

**shell-shocked**   upset because of a sudden, terrible event   p. 25

**stereotyped**   treated as if everyone in a certain group is exactly alike   p. 46

**strenuous**   needing great effort   p. 69

**surge**   a sudden rise   p. 6

# T

**typical**   a good example of something   p. 38

# U

**unattended**   not watched or not taken care of   p. 14

**uninspired**   not showing any creativity or excitement   p. 88

# V

**villain**   the most important bad character in a movie or story   p. 57

**violence**   forceful actions that cause harm to people or objects   p. 58

# My Personal Dictionary

_____

_____

_____

_____

_____

_____

_____

_____

_____

_____

_____

_____

_____

_____

# My Personal Dictionary

# Writing Checklist

**1.** I followed the directions for writing.

**2.** My writing shows that I read and understood the article.

**3.** I capitalized the names of people.

**4.** I capitalized the proper names of places and things.

**5.** I read my writing aloud and listened for missing words.

**6.** I used a dictionary to check words that don't look right.

◆ **Use the chart below to check off the things on the list that you have done.**

| ✓ | Lesson Numbers | | | | | | | | |
|---|---|---|---|---|---|---|---|---|---|
| **Checklist Numbers** | **1** | **2** | **3** | **4** | **5** | **6** | **7** | **8** | **9** |
| **1.** | | | | | | | | | |
| **2.** | | | | | | | | | |
| **3.** | | | | | | | | | |
| **4.** | | | | | | | | | |
| **5.** | | | | | | | | | |
| **6.** | | | | | | | | | |

# Progress Check

You can take charge of your own progress. The Comprehension and Critical Thinking Progress Graph on the next page can help you. Use it to keep track of how you are doing as you work through the lessons in this book. Check the graph often with your teacher. What types of skills cause you trouble? Talk with your teacher about ways to work on these.

A sample Comprehension and Critical Thinking Progress Graph is shown below. The first three lessons have been filled in to show you how to use the graph.

## Sample Comprehension and Critical Thinking Progress Graph

◆ **Directions:** Write your percentage score for each lesson in the box under the number of the lesson. Then put a small X on the line. The X goes above the number of the lesson and across from the score you earned. Chart your progress by drawing a line to connect the Xs.

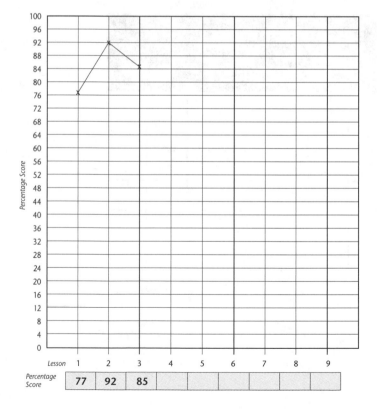

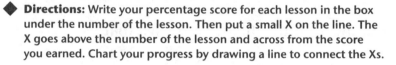

# Comprehension and Critical Thinking Progress Graph

◆ **Directions:** Write your percentage score for each lesson in the box under the number of the lesson. Then put a small X on the line. The X goes above the number of the lesson and across from the score you earned. Chart your progress by drawing a line to connect the Xs.

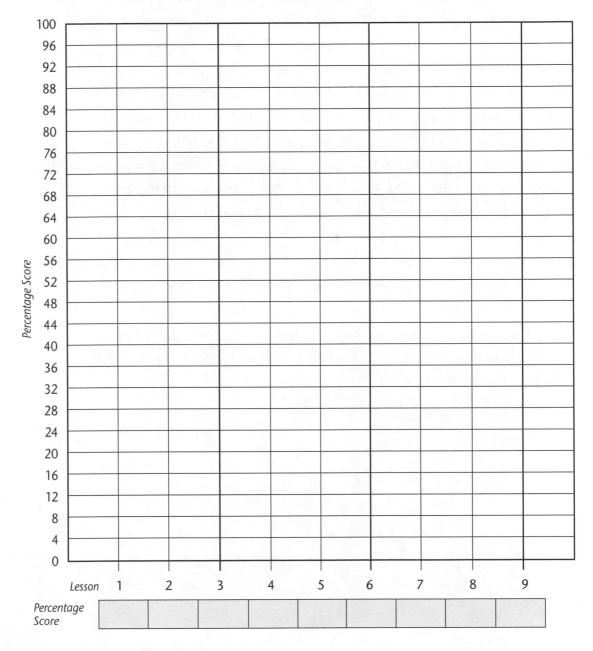

# Photo Credits